Westonbirt
The National Arboretum

Text by **Tony Russell**
Photography by **Derek Harris**

 A Friends of Westonbirt Arboretum Publication

In Robert Holford's personal copy of Bacon's Essays, the following passage was found to be specially marked by him.

"God Almighty first planted a garden......and indeed it is the purest of human pleasures......I do hold it there ought to be gardens for all months of the year, in which, severally, things of beauty may be then in season......that you may have *ver perpetuum*".

Francis Bacon

CONTENTS

INTRODUCTION

For nearly 200 years Westonbirt has been home to some of the worlds most exotic species of temperate trees and shrubs amassed by the Holford family, who created the Arboretum. Starting in the heyday of the great Victorian plant hunters they were fired with a passion to collect and show them to their guests. Holford's genius was in his skill and imagination to plant with such foresight knowing he would never see the mature results in his lifetime. Thanks to careful husbandry by the family until the onset of the 2nd World War in 1939 and the Forestry Commission since 1956, this is the legacy that our generations now enjoy.

The Arboretum is part of a much larger historic landscape, bisected by the main Tetbury to Bath road. It comprised the mansion, (now Westonbirt School), pleasure gardens and parkland. Despite fragmented ownership, this has survived virtually unchanged and is registered as a Grade 1 Listed Landscape on the English Heritage's 'Register of Parks and Gardens of Special Historical Interest'.

The Arboretum is a place for all seasons and this guide sets out to lead the visitor through the year. Tony Russell is an unashamed enthusiast who was Westonbirt Head Forester for thirteen years before leaving to bring his passion for trees to a wider audience through his writing and broadcasting. In this guide he writes with an intimate knowledge and love of the Arboretum which is complimented by the stunning award winning photography of Derek Harris, one of Britain's finest landscape photographers. Together they trace back two thousand years to the Small-leaved Lime and the medieval woodland management in Silk Wood through to Holford's first plantings and the development of the Arboretum into one of the world's greatest tree collections.

This is not just a recreational showpiece but is also a living laboratory, a centre of research and education geared for the serious student, schoolchild and visitor. Additions to the collection continue to be made. Conservation is of particular importance e.g. endangered species, are propagated and nurtured with the possibility for future reintroduction to their native habitat.

Finally there is fun and celebration too for the visitor with concerts, exhibitions, Sculptree festival and the now famous illuminated trail in the pre Christmas weekends.

The guide is not conclusive and leaves plenty of scope to discover the delights of more magnificent trees and the rich flora and fauna inhabiting the 600 acres. Above all and in every season it is a place to enjoy peace and solitude at the very heart of nature.

We owe a huge debt of gratitude to the Forestry Commission management team at Westonbirt. Their painstaking work and dedication is recognised throughout the world. We thank them too for their willing co-operation in the publication of this guide. As Friends of Westonbirt our constant aim is to support the Forestry Commission in all this vital work for the environment and to enhance the appreciation and enjoyment for everyone.

Hugh Purkess, Chairman - Friends of Westonbirt Arboretum

Opposite: Palmer Ride in spring

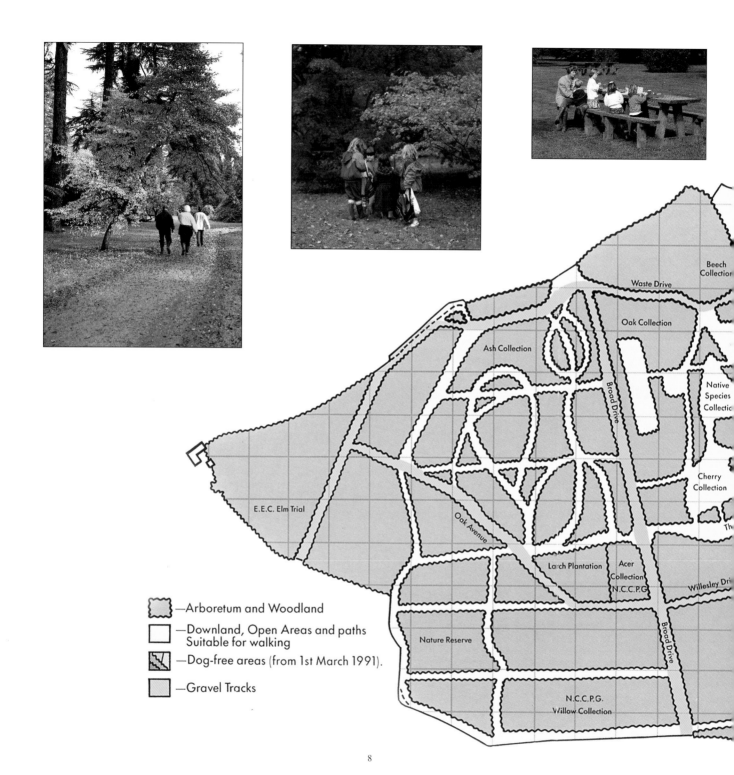

—Arboretum and Woodland

—Downland, Open Areas and paths Suitable for walking

—Dog-free areas (from 1st March 1991).

—Gravel Tracks

Beech Collection

Waste Drive

Oak Collection

Ash Collection

Broad Drive

Native Species Collection

Cherry Collection

E.E.C. Elm Trial

Oak Avenue

Th

Larch Plantation

Acer Collection
N.C.C.P.G.

Willesley Dri

Nature Reserve

Broad Drive

N.C.C.P.G.
Willow Collection

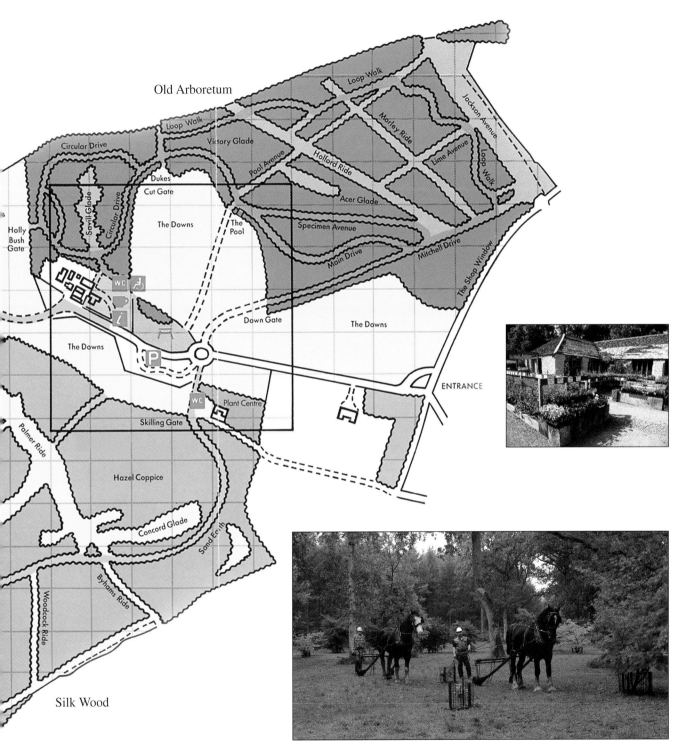

Old Arboretum

Loop Walk

Jackson Avenue

Morley Ride

Lime Avenue

Loop Walk

Loop Walk

Victory Glade

Circular Drive

Pool Avenue

Holford Ride

Acer Glade

Dukes
Cut Gate

Savill Glade

Circular Drive

Specimen Avenue

Holly
Bush
Gate

The Downs

The
Pool

Main Drive

Mitchell Drive

The Shop Window

WC

i

The Downs

Down Gate

The Downs

P

The Downs

ENTRANCE

WC

Plant Centre

Skilling Gate

Palmer Ride

Hazel Coppice

Concord Glade

Sand Earth

Byhams Ride

Woodcock Ride

Silk Wood

9

WESTONBIRT FACTS

Created	1829 by Robert Stayner Holford
Present Owner	Forestry Commission
Location	Three miles south of Tetbury, Gloucestershire on the A433 Grid reference: ST 854 900
Elevation	120 metres (400 feet) above sea level
Average rainfall	850mm (34 inches)
Area	240 hectares (600 acres)
Footpaths	27kms (17 miles)
Total specimens in collection	18,500
Total taxa (Different types) in collection	3,900
Oldest	Small-leaved Lime, *Tilia cordata,* approximately 2000 years old
Tallest	Giant redwood *Sequoiadendron giganteum,* 47 metres (153feet)
Red data species (rare, endangered, extinct)	109 taxa
Champion trees (biggest of their kind in UK)	104 taxa
National Collections	Salix (willow) 260 taxa Acer (maple) Japanese cultivars 180 taxa
Visitors	300,000 per annum
Silk Wood	Believed to be a derivation of the name Soake, a 9th century Saxon chief who held land in this area
Opening Hours	Grounds open all year from 10am until 8pm or dusk if earlier

THE HISTORY OF WESTONBIRT

There is a stone in the Corinium Museum, Cirencester, upon which is an inscription to the memory of a Roman named Mettus. The stone dates from around 375 AD and was ploughed up in a field close to Westonbirt in the early 1800's. It is believed to be the earliest evidence of human settlement in the Westonbirt area.

The earliest written information on the area comes from the Domesday Book of 1086. Here, there are references to two manors at Weston during the reign of Edward the Confessor (1042-1066). Both manors comprised of arable and meadow land, one was held by Elnod, the other by Bricsi, both Saxons.

The name Weston derives from the fact that the manors were located west of the Roman 'Bowl Down' Road and in the western extremity of the Longtree Hundred; one of the forty or so hundreds, (areas of land), into which the County of Gloucestershire was divided.

After the Conquest, both manors were given to the Norman, Earl Hugh of Chester who built the original parish church. In 1215 the combined manor passed to Maurice de Gaunt, and then to Hugh le Bret shortly afterwards. It stayed with the le Bret family for one hundred years and in 1309 there is the first recorded use of the name Weston Birt, (Birt, undoubtedly deriving from the name of The Lords of the Manor). It remained like this until the twentieth century, when the two words were combined into the current Westonbirt.

The Elizabethan Manor House

The Holford Era

It wasn't until the mid 1600s that the Holford family, creators of much of the landscape and buildings we see around us today, became associated with Weston Birt. In 1654, at the tender age of five, Sarah Crewe inherited the manor, (which now included an Elizabethan manor house), from her father John Crewe. In 1665 she met and married Richard Holford, a Barrister-in-Law.

Richard Holford was a descendant of an ancient Cheshire family who could trace their ancestry back to the Norman Ricardus de Runchamp, who owned land near Plumley in Cheshire. The family had assumed the name Holford in 1316 from the name of a small hamlet on their land just to the west of Plumley. 'Holford' actually means, 'the lower water crossing' and in this particular instance, the water referred to is the Wincham Brook.

On 28th June 1694, Richard Holford was knighted. Although based in London, he made regular visits to Weston Birt, until his death in 1714. During this period, many improvements were made to the estate, including the building of a new farm, barns, stables, coach house and granary. The Dew Pond, situated close to Pool Gate in the Old Arboretum, very likely dates from this period.

In 1753 Sir Richard's grandson Peter Holford became Governor and major shareholder of the recently formed New River Company, which supplied London with its first piped, clean water supply. The company was based at Stoke Newington, North London, and took its name (and water) from the New River, which flows southwards from Enfield into the capital. Some of the company's original reservoirs and waterworks buildings are still in existence in the Stoke Newington area, along with a notable collection of trees in the local cemetery, which are believed to have been planted by the Holford's.

It was the dramatic rise in the value of the shares of the New River Company that underpinned the family's wealth.

Peter died in 1803 and was succeeded by his second son, George Peter Holford. In 1818, George demolished the Elizabethan manor house, which had stood directly to the east of Weston Birt church, on the site currently covered by terracing. A map of 1810 shows a garden to the north of the manor encompassing the site of the present-day school. The only remnant from that garden is a large yew tree which stands on the southern edge of the main school lawn. It is believed to be over 400 years old, and legend has it that milk for the manor house was kept cool in buckets hung from its lower boughs. George replaced the Elizabethan manor with a Regency Gothic villa in 1823.

Birth of the Arboretum

In 1839, George Peter Holford died and was succeeded by his only child, Robert Stayner Holford, who was then 31 years old. For at least ten years prior to his father's death, Robert had been active on the estate. He graduated from Oriel College, Oxford, in 1829 and planted the very first trees of the Arboretum in that same year. It was a time of great excitement in the horticultural world. David Douglas had just returned from his second plant hunting expedition to America, introducing more than 210 new species to Britain, including arboreal giants such as the Douglas Fir, *Pseudotsuga menziesii* and the Western Yellow Pine, *Pinus Ponderosa*.

On his return to London, Douglas was proclaimed a hero and it is very likely that Robert Holford would have been aware of this and became inspired to start his own collection of these botanical rarities at Weston Birt. There is still today, at least one original Douglas introduction in the Arboretum, a Monterey Pine, *Pinus Radiata,* from California, which stands at the junction of Main and Circular Drives.

Robert Stayner Holford (1808 - 1892)

Robert Holford chose to start his collection on an area of downland approximately one mile to the west of the house. It is said that he chose this spot because, as he walked across what was then open fields, he saw the rich sandy loam soil which was being brought to the surface by badgers opening up new setts. Today, we know this area as Savill Glade, or Down Covert and many of Holford's original 1829 plantings are still growing here. Ring counts on mature trees which have died in this area, all date back to this period.

As far as we know, Robert Holford never actively took part in overseas plant-hunting expeditions, although it has been suggested that he may well have financed some. This is perfectly possible, as he had accrued an enormous wealth. In 1838 his bachelor uncle Robert died, leaving him several properties and over £1,000,000. There was also a dramatic recovery of bullion which had been buried by an ancestor on the Isle of Wight during the threat of Napoleonic invasion. Then in 1839, on the death of his father, he inherited the Weston Birt estate as well.

Weston Birt House

The next forty years saw a period of almost frenetic activity with much of the original estate changing out of all recognition. In 1839, Robert Holford employed the Italian architect Lewis Vulliamy to expand and make improvements to the Regency Gothic villa. In 1840, work started on the Park and Pleasure Grounds surrounding the villa. These were considered to be two very distinct features, but both reflected the 'Picturesque' style of the day. The Park was designed as a 'natural' open landscape, interspersed with carefully placed individual, or groups of trees, which helped focus the eye to the vista beyond. The Pleasure Grounds, by contrast, were highly cultivated, with lawns, ornamental plantings and architecture. It is very likely Holford was influenced and advised by garden landscape designer William Sawrey Gilpin, who had published the highly successful book '*Practical Hints upon Landscape Gardening*' in 1832.

In 1843 Henry Edward Hamlen, a pupil of Vulliamy, was engaged to help develop the Pleasure Grounds. He designed and built the 'Italian Garden' with its sumptuous domed pavilions. This was followed shortly by the rockery, grotto, hot-houses for orchid cultivation, the kitchen gardens and the Mercury garden.

Today, the Pleasure Grounds are not associated with the Arboretum but are part of the grounds managed by Westonbirt School. They are open to the public several times throughout the year. Part of the original Park laid out by Holford is now Westonbirt Golf Course.

'Italian Garden' - today

Mercury Statue

Dorchester House

In 1849 Robert acquired the freehold to the old Dorchester House in Park Lane, London, whereupon he commissioned its re-building by Vulliamy.

Back at Weston Birt, Robert's next project, in 1853 was to create two new drives, lodges and gates. At the same time he had the level of the road between the arboretum and the house lowered, so carriages using it did not interrupt his view. This is still evident today when one stands on Holford Ride and looks towards the house. In 1854 Holford turned his attention to the village, which lay immediately to the south and west of the Norman church. It was clear that if he wished to extend his Pleasure Grounds in that direction, he would need to move the village! Robert did just that, leaving only the church in place.

In the same year, Robert married Mary Anne, daughter of General James Lindsay MP, of Balcarres, Fife, and was himself elected as Conservative MP for East Gloucestershire.

By 1858, the houses that comprise the present village had been completed and villagers installed. The old village pond had become a lake set within 40 glorious acres of landscaped grounds and the church, re-built and restored by Vulliamy, had been absorbed into Holford's Pleasure Grounds like some decorative folly.

By this time, Holford had already made plans to replace the Regency Gothic villa built by his father. Work began in 1863 with, once again, Vulliamy as Principle Architect for the new house. It was modelled on the late Renaissance mansion, Wollaton Hall in Nottinghamshire, and took until 1870 to complete. It was and still is, a magnificent building. Constructed of Cotswold stone from several quarries in the Weston Birt area, and faced with Bath stone, it has a frontage measuring 110m (360 ft) in length. Inside, there were 62 bedrooms, 11 bathrooms, a Royal suite (members of the Royal Family were frequent visitors), a theatre with a stage, a conservatory 9m (30ft) high, libraries, studies, drawing rooms, a billiard room, dining rooms and a grand galleried hall. It also included all the latest 'mod-cons'. There was warm-air background heating and a high-pressure water supply to power the organ, the lift and Mrs. Holford's bidet! Total cost for the building was around £250,000. At the same time, immediately outside the house, Holford was building up extensive collections of amaryllis and orchids in a whole series of newly constructed glasshouses.

Westonbirt House as it is today

The Tree Collection

It would be expected with all this activity that, Robert Holford would have had little time for his tree collection. In fact, quite the opposite was true. Exotic trees and shrubs were finding their way to Weston Birt from all around the temperate world. There are suggestions that in some instances even the soil they had been growing in was imported along with the plant! The majority were planted in the Arboretum, but many ended up in Holford's Pleasure Grounds and some in the parkland beyond. Whilst some of these plants came directly to Weston Birt from overseas plant hunting expeditions, many came as part of informal exchanges with other collectors in Great Britain, including the Earl of Ducie at Tortworth Court and Earl Somers at Eastnor Castle.

Virtually no direct Holford records of these plantings have ever been found. However, Holford's Head Gardener from 1831 until 1868, Jonah Neale, kept extensive details within his diaries. One of his most interesting entries relates to the Giant Redwood or Wellingtonia, *Sequoiadendron giganteum…. "September 13th 1854, Mr Holford bought four plants from Mr. James Veitch, Kings Road, Chelsea, London. The four plants cost £6….. In March 1856 two of them were planted on each side of the entrance gate to the Arboretum opposite the new lodges"*. One was planted by Robert Holford, and one by his wife Mary. Both trees are still in existence today and what is particularly interesting is the source of the seed. The first ever seeds of the American Giant Redwood to arrive in England came via the Cornish plant collector William Lobb in December 1853. All the seed went to Veitch's nursery in Chelsea, who had commissioned

Lobb's expedition. So the plants purchased, raised and eventually planted as saplings by the lodge gates at Weston Birt, are original introductions.

By 1855 much of the landscape we enjoy today had been laid out, including Main Drive, Specimen Avenue, and the three rides which radiate off the main house, namely Holford Ride, Morley Ride and Jackson Avenue. Interestingly, the Arboretum was laid out in the 'Picturesque' style, much like the Park and the Pleasure Grounds. Trees were not grouped in a systematic scientific or geographical way but rather more for aesthetic appeal.

Sir George Lindsay Holford K.C.V.O (1860 - 1926)

Sir George Holford

Robert Holford and his wife Mary had three daughters born 1855-58. Three Giant Redwoods which still stand at the south-western end of Mitchell Drive, were planted by the girls and are affectionately known today as the 'Three Sisters'. In 1860 they had a son, George Lindsay Holford, who played a rather bigger part in the development of the Arboretum. By the age of fifteen, he was already helping his father with the planting. Indeed, it is George who is credited with the creation of the original Acer Glade and the expansion of the collection across the valley into Silk Wood. Both of these major developments took place in the mid 1870's.

Robert Holford died in 1892. By any standards, he was a remarkable man. He was a great collector, not only of plants, but also of art and books. At the time of his death, his orchid collection was considered to be one of the finest in the country.

Over the next 34 years, George Holford continued expanding the Arboretum. However, much of his time was spent at Court as he was appointed Equerry-in-Waiting to the Prince of Wales in 1892, remaining in his service after the Prince became Edward VII in 1901. After Edward VII's death in 1910, George was knighted and became Equerry-in-Waiting to Her Majesty Queen Alexandra and Extra Equerry to King George V. It was during this period that members of the Royal Family were regular visitors to 'Westonbirt'.

One of the major contributions made by Sir George to the Arboretum, was the planting of spectacular collections of rhododendrons and azaleas in the areas known today as Savill Glade in the Old Arboretum and Sand Earth in Silk Wood. Many of these were hybrids developed by Sir George and his staff in 'secret nurseries' hidden within the grounds. Some plants however, were original introductions by plant collectors of the day, including Ernest Wilson. Sir George is known to have contributed to Wilson's Chinese expedition of 1910. Many introductions from this particular expedition were planted at Westonbirt.

In 1912 at the age of 52, Sir George married Sarah Menzies in St. James' Palace, London, in front of a congregation which included King George V and Queen Mary.

It was in orchid cultivation that Sir George acquired world renown. His partner in this work was Mr. H.G.Alexander whom he appointed in 1899. Between them, they cultivated orchids which became favourites throughout the world. Perhaps the greatest recognition was the award of the King's Cup at the 1912 Royal Horticultural Society International Show for a breathtaking exhibition of Westonbirt orchids. The success of this show was the catalyst for the RHS creating the first Chelsea Flower Show the following year. In 1913, Sir George presented over 200 orchids to Kew, many of them new cultivars raised within some of his 27 orchid houses at Westonbirt. The Royal Horticultural Society still awards annually the Westonbirt Orchid Medal for outstanding achievements in the orchid world.

In 1921, Sir George Holford commissioned the renowned botanist, A. Bruce Jackson to compile the first inventory of the Westonbirt collection. His monumental work, entitled 'Trees and Shrubs at Westonbirt' was published in early 1927. Sir George never saw its completion for on the 11th September 1926, he died at the age of 66.

After the Holfords

Sir George had no children so the estate passed to his nephew, the Right Hon. Edmund Robert, Fourth Earl of Morley. The Morleys already owned a large estate at Saltram, near Plymouth, and within months, both Dorchester House in London and Westonbirt House, along with its contents, 550 acres of parkland and several outlying farms and cottages were up for sale by auction. The auction failed to secure a purchaser for Westonbirt House, and so the house was sold privately to the Revd. P.E.Warrington, Vicar of Monkton Combe, Somerset. He bought it on behalf of the Martyr's Memorial and Church of England Trust to establish a girl's public school which opened on 11th May 1928.

The Arboretum and Silk Wood were never part of this sale. Lord Morley had a great interest in horticulture and placed both under the supervision of the respected plantsman W. J. Mitchell. For the next 30 years, Lord Morley regularly visited Westonbirt and carried out some limited planting of his own. Gone however were the days of unlimited money and labour, due in part to World War II.

Lord Morley died in 1951. The Arboretum and Silk Wood passed to his brother the Fifth Earl of Morley. By this time neglect was apparent in many parts of the Arboretum and several of the specimens recorded in Jackson's inventory had died. In 1956 the family gave the Arboretum to the Government's National Land Fund. An article in Country Life, by A.G.L. Hellyer, around this time, captured perfectly the uncertain future of the Arboretum….. *"and so finally to Westonbirt…..the noble Arboretum commenced by Robert Holford and completed by Lord Morley, the fate of which now hangs in the balance. Is it to become the property of the Forestry Commission and, if so, will its many unique and beautiful, but presumably quite useless, trees be preserved as they ought? No one seems to know the answers to these questions, and I sometimes have the feeling that not enough people care. But, if the heritage of Westonbirt is neglected, one may be sure that both we and our children will be the poorer"*.

The Arboretum and Silk Wood were handed over, as a scientific collection, to the Forestry Commission and placed under the supervision of the internationally renown dendrologist Alan Mitchell. An Advisory Committee was established and Research Forester Edward Leyshon, appointed as Manager. Over the next five years extensive remedial and restoration work took place and during 1961, through the felling of yew trees in Down Covert, Savill Glade was created to a design by Eric Savill of Windsor.

Also in 1961, the Forestry Commission officially opened Westonbirt to the public for the first time and in 1966, under the direction of Edward Leyshon, a new Acer Glade was created alongside the original Glade planted by Robert and Sir George Holford ninety years before.

Since then, through the dedication, expertise and sheer hard work of the Forestry Commission and its staff, Westonbirt Arboretum has thrived. Much of this work is described within this book under the section 'Westonbirt Today'.

It is true to say that the collection is as well cared for today as at any time in its history, thus ensuring this remarkable Holford legacy lives on

Spring

Ask anyone what they know of Westonbirt Arboretum and inevitably the word autumn will arise. Westonbirt has become the place to view the dramatic leaf colour prelude to winter.

By comparison, springtime at Westonbirt is relatively unknown and yet for those who have discovered the secret, it is a time of great beauty and enchantment.

The season begins quietly beneath the ancient oaks of Silk Wood. Here, thousands of butter-cream coloured hazel catkins, dripping from bare branches, are warmed by the early spring sun. This warmth ripens the catkins, helping to release clouds of pollen which drift through the rays of sunshine before settling, like fine dust, upon the emerging leaves below.

Magnolia sprengeri 'Diva'

This is wild Westonbirt. Silk Wood dates back long before the arrival of the Holfords and their Victorian creation. Much of this woodland has been here for at least 600 years and probably far longer. There is at least one tree, a Small-leaved Lime, *Tilia cordata,* just off Broad Drive, which is believed to be over 2000 years old. For centuries the hazel has been coppiced (cut down to the stump) and used to make sheep hurdles, which helped to pen Cotswold sheep as they methodically grazed the tops of the wolds.

As February turns to March, Silk Wood is set ablaze with a glorious mix of yellows, creams and whites, as celandines, primroses and wood anemones burst into flower. This is their moment to perform and they need to flower and set seed quickly before the oak leaf canopy overhead closes cover, bringing six months of shade to the woodland.

In the Old Arboretum, some of the more exotic members of the collection are stirring from their winter slumber. Great grey, hairy magnolia buds swell daily before, seemingly overnight, clothing whole trees in a mass of pink or white flowers. Two of Westonbirt's finest magnolias are also the first to flower, the Pink Tulip Tree, *Magnolia campbelii* and the Goddess Magnolia, *Magnolia sprengeri* 'Diva'. Both originate from Asia and both can be found flowering in Savill Glade in late March to mid April. *Magnolia campbellii* is normally the first to flower. It has pale pink, goblet-like flowers, which, when fully open, are the size of tea plates. *Magnolia sprengeri* 'Diva' has slightly smaller flowers, but what it lacks in size it makes up for in colour. The blooms are a superb deep pink, and they cover the tree from head to foot. The specimen which stands at the southern end of Savill Glade is, at 27 metres (90 feet),

Opposite: The Link in Spring

Azaleas in Savill Glade

Circular Drive

the tallest in Britain. Only planted in 1960, it has grown on average a phenomenal 60 cms (2 ft) every year since planting.

Westonbirt is situated approximately 130 metres (420 ft) above sea level, on an exposed ridge of Oolithic limestone, not, you may think, the best environment for establishing a premier plant collection. However, to combat this exposure, Robert Holford planted hundreds of hardy British trees, such as oak, yew, Scots Pine and holly to provide shelter for his more exotic introductions.

Nowhere is this more evident than along Circular Drive. Combine this with rich acid soil, which overlies the limestone in some places to a depth of 2 metres (6ft 6in), and you have almost perfect growing conditions for camellias, rhododendrons and azaleas. In springtime, there are few places in Britain to rival the magnificent flowering displays of this area. Rose-pink camellias, such as 'Bow Bells' and 'Donation', both hybrids raised by J. C. Williams at Caerhays Castle in Cornwall, sit perfectly alongside the showy pink-white bicoloured, camellia 'Harlequin'. In all, there are over fifty different camellia cultivars at Westonbirt providing a stunning spring feature. In truth, however, these are just the 'warm-up act' for the rhododendron show about to begin.

By mid-April, the show is in full swing. The diversity is extreme, ranging from the small, but exquisite, *Rhododendron cinnabarinum* with its waxy red tubular flowers, and the beautiful pure white, spotted with green, flowers of *Rhododendron quinquefolium* through to the almost rude vigour of the giant-leaved rhododendrons such as *sinogrande*, *fictolacteum* and *calophytum*.

It is not only Circular Drive that has all the fun, there are spectacular flowering rhododendrons to be

Spring coloured acer in The Link

Bluebells in The Link

Prunus x yedoensis 'Shidare Yoshino'

Deciduous Azaleas on Circular Drive

seen in the appropriately named Sand Earth, close to Willesley Drive in Silk Wood. Here, the feeling is less formal, with tongues of native woodland providing a fine backdrop to such show stoppers as the sweetly-scented creamy-white flowers of *Rhododendron griffithianum*.

Probably one of the most remarked upon rhododendrons at Westonbirt is found on Main Drive. It is called *Rhododendron williamsianum*, and has small heart-shaped leaves with delightful single pink, bell-shaped flowers. What makes it of great interest to many visitors, is its size. It is relatively slow growing and an ideal plant for a small garden or even a container.

In the same area as *Rhododendron williamsianum*, there are two fine specimens of the flowering cherry *Prunus* 'Tai-Haku', the 'Great White Cherry'. If you are lucky enough to catch them in flower, normally towards the end of April, you are in for a real treat. The flowers are pure white, almost 5 cms (2 ins) across, and surrounded by emerging young coppery-red leaves. The effect is quite simply beautiful. Westonbirt's cherry collection is spread throughout the Old Arboretum and Silk Wood. A springtime walk in almost any direction will reveal blossoming splendour. For sheer perfection however, head for Silk Wood in late April or early May. Here the Cherry Blossom combines magnificently with great swathes of bluebells. Although brief, bluebell time has to be one of the loveliest times of all to visit Westonbirt.

One of the best areas to catch this display is The Link in Silk Wood. A long, secluded glade, planted with Japanese Maples and bordered by ancient semi-natural woodland on either side. Take any path through this woodland and you will be surrounded by carpets of purple-blue haze and the most delightful fragrance.

By mid-May, springtime flowering is reaching its peak. Along Circular Drive, Pool Avenue and throughout Savill Glade, the air is heady with the scent from deciduous azaleas in full flower. The range of colours is remarkable. Bright red, orange and apricot intermingle with more subtle lemon, cream and white. It is the paler colours that produce the stronger fragrances, heightened by the increasing warmth of the sun.

Late flowering magnolias, such as *Magnolia wilsonii* and *Magnolia sieboldii* add to the fragrance. Their flowers are delightful with fresh white sepals set off dramatically by bright crimson stamens. They would probably take the prize for 'Best in Show' were it not for one tree about to take centre stage. The 'Pocket-handkerchief Tree', *Davidia involucrata* is without doubt one of the most beautiful trees of the world. The 'Champion Tree', (tallest in Britain) is found close to Main Drive in the Old Arboretum at Westonbirt. It is over 25 metres (80 ft) tall and when in flower, in May, it always draws a crowd who marvel at the way it is draped in large papery-white bracts. It was first introduced into Britain in 1904 by Ernest Wilson. Born in Chipping Campden, Gloucestershire, he is considered to be one of the finest plant collectors of all time.

As spring draws to a close, it is well worth taking a stroll across the open downland which separates the Old Arboretum from Silk Wood. Here, particularly on the slopes, you will find a whole wealth of wild flowers including Common Spotted and Bee Orchids. Perhaps not as showy as the exotic magnolia and rhododendron collections, they are nonetheless a beautiful part of Westonbirt's springtime experience.

Davidia involucrata

Rhododendron

Paulownia tomentosa

Deciduous azalea

Magnolia stellata

Deciduous azalea

Camellia

Rhododendron

Magnolia x wiesenerii

Summer

After the urgency and exuberance of spring, a Westonbirt summer is a far more gentle affair. It is a time for reflection, time to relax in some leafy, shady glade and soak up the peace and tranquillity which is so much a part of this beautiful place. Gone are the massed floral displays, replaced by botanical gems that are more subtle in their flowering. Somehow this coyness makes them even more enjoyable when found.

One such gem is the early summer flowering Judas Tree – *Cercis siliquastrum*. Clusters of rosy-lilac flowers clothe the branches right back to the main stem. The finest specimen at Westonbirt is on Main Drive in the Old Arboretum. It takes its name from Judas Iscariot, who is said to have hung himself from the tree after betraying Christ.

As midsummer's day approaches, so the flowering dogwoods reach their best. *Cornus kousa*, the Japanese Dogwood, is one of the finest. Rather like the Pocket-handkerchief Tree, *Davidia involucrata*, the flowers are insignificant, but they are surrounded by showy white bracts which stand erect above its spreading branches. The best display at Westonbirt comes from a group which grow alongside Waste Drive in Silk Wood.

Judas Tree *Cercis siliquastrum*

Also in Silk Wood, on Willesley Drive, there are several superb specimens of the Manna Ash, *Fraxinus ornus*. In June, this beautiful tree produces heavily scented creamy-white plumes of flower which are adored by bees. It originates from Southern Europe where it is commercially grown in orchards for its sap. When the tree is tapped, the sap crystallizes to form mannitol, a sweet, mildly alcoholic substance, which is used as a sugar substitute in diabetic food.

As the sun reaches its zenith, so one of the world's most beautiful trees comes into flower. The Indian Horse Chestnut, *Aesculus indica*, grows wild from Northern India into the Himalayas. Although it is related to the Common Horse Chestnut, which adorns our parks and gardens with flowering splendour in spring time, the Indian Horse Chestnut waits until it can put in a 'solo performance' in early July. It is an event worth waiting for. The flowers, almost orchid-like in appearance, are pink and white with yellow markings. They are grouped together on upright stalks surrounded by dark olive-green leaves and the effect is stunning. There are several good specimens to be seen on Loop Walk, Main Drive and Pool Avenue in the Old Arboretum.

It is during the summer that several events of a less botanical nature take place at

Opposite: Silk Wood

Lime Avenue

Smoke bush *Cotinus coggygria* on Mitchell Drive

The Downs

The Link

Westonbirt. Ranging from concerts to festivals and plays, they span the period from early June through to the end of August.

The first is the unique International Festival of Gardens, which brings together twenty contemporary show gardens with an emphasis on original art and design concepts. Running throughout the summer, it provides fresh ideas on how we can develop our own gardens in the twenty-first century.

At the end of July it is the time for the Westonbirt Classical Concert with Fireworks. This superb event takes place in front of a sell-out audience of 6,000 who picnic beneath the stars while listening to some of the better known classics played by the English National Orchestra. The evening's climax is a 'Last Night of the Proms' finale, accompanied by a spectacular firework display.

Westonbirt's final summer event is the 'Festival of Wood'. This three-day festival is centred around 'Sculptree', an amazing display of giant woodcarving. Twelve wood carvers use chainsaws to turn large tree trunks into incredible sculpture, which is then auctioned for charity – normally on August bank holiday Monday.

With all this activity, one could be forgiven for forgetting about the real stars of Westonbirt, and they are, of course, the trees and shrubs. A walk through the Old Arboretum anytime during high summer will soon solve that.

One of Westonbirt's most unsung displays comes from the flowering hydrangeas. There are groups to be found on Circular Drive, Loop Walk and in Victory Glade, a delightful shady glade between Main Drive and Pool Avenue. Here, great clumps

International Festival of Gardens 'The Renaissance Garden'

'Sculptree' at The Festival of Wood

Mop-head hydrangea

Indian Bean Tree *Catalpa bignonioides*

Tulip Tree *Liriodendron tulipifera*

Early purple orchid

Wild flowers

Butterfly orchid

Chilean firebush *Embothrium coccineum*

Japanses Dogwood *Cornus kousa*

Autumn crocus *Colchicum autumnale*

of both mop-head and lacecap flowers range in colour from pure white to the deepest blue. One of the most striking is *Hydrangea aspera* which carries magnificent heads of pale porcelain-blue flowers with an outer ring of lilac-pink florets.

Not far from Victory Glade is Lime Avenue, one of Robert Holfords greatest creations. This splendid feature, containing over thirty mature lime trees, *Tilia x europaea,* runs between Jackson Avenue and Holford Ride. On a hot summer's day, beneath the canopy, the air is cool and the shadows strong. During flowering time in July, the sound is also quite deafening from thousands of bees, busy collecting nectar from vast quantities of fragrant blossom which hangs from every bough.

Jackson Avenue is made up of limes, cedars and the American Tulip Tree, *Liriodendron tulipifera.* One of the largest exotic trees ever introduced into Britain, the Tulip Tree is also one of the most distinctive. The leaves look like someone has taken a pair of scissors to them and cut the top off and the flowers are out of this world! They are tulip-like in appearance, greenish yellow in colour, with glorious rich orange markings. The only problem in Jackson Avenue is that they are all 20 metres (65ft) above head height, such are the size of the trees! However, in Savill Glade, close to the Great Oak Hall, there are specimens with low hanging branches which produce flowers at eye level.

Not to be outdone by its fellow American, the Indian Bean Tree, *Catalpa bignonioides* produces beautiful white, speckled with yellow and purple flowers in summer. Although fairly common throughout southern England, the assumption by many people is that it originates from the Indian sub-continent. In fact, the Indian reference is actually the Native American Indians who used to dry the beans, (which appear in long runner bean-like pods after flowering), paint them and wear them as neck decorations.

Throughout Westonbirt, there are several excellent specimens of the Smoke Bush *Cotinus coggygria.* The name comes from the smoky-pink-grey flowers which hang like halos around its translucent oval leaves. Although the species has green leaves, many cultivars have been developed which have purple or burgundy coloured leaves. Fine specimens of both can be found on Mitchell Drive in the Old Arboretum and Broad Drive in Silk Wood.

On the more acid soil areas, such as Circular Drive, close to where the rhododendrons perform in the spring, there are several small evergreen trees which, for most of the year are passed by without a second glance. However, in late summer, they suddenly spring into life. These are *Eucryphias*, and in particular *Eucryphia x nymansensis*, named after the famous garden Nymans, in Sussex. For three short weeks towards the end of summer, they bear exquisite delicate white flowers which have a fragrance like no other. On hot sunny days, this heady scent drifts along Circular Drive intoxicating all who walk there.

Almost the final act of a Westonbirt summer is the appearance of the leafless lilac-pink flowers of the Autumn crocus or Meadow Saffron, *Colchicum autumnale.* They sparkle like gems amidst dry brown grass throughout Silk Wood, particularly along Palmer Ride and in glades close to The Link. As the nights begin to cool and early morning dew glistens upon their delicate petals, it is clear that summer's glass is empty, and a Westonbirt autumn is about to begin.

Autumn

Autumn is without doubt the most popular time of year to visit Westonbirt. Close on 150,000 people visit during a six week period from early October until mid November. They arrive to experience one of nature's most dramatic displays, the spectacular leaf colour change which signals the end of the growing season and the approaching dormancy of winter. The diversity and vibrancy of leaf colours to be found at Westonbirt are unsurpassed in Britain. Combine this with fruits, hips and berries in profusion, and you have the makings of a botanical experience like no other.

One of the first trees to turn colour is the Full-moon Maple, *Acer japonicum* 'Vitifolium'. There are several magnificent specimens to be found at Westonbirt,

including one on Jackson Avenue in the Old Arboretum, and three on Willesley Drive in Silk Wood. However, the finest of them all is on Holford Ride, not far from the junction with Pool Avenue. It is a tree frequented by Westonbirt's foresters every year in early autumn as they try to gauge the vibrancy of the colour climax about to begin. For no two autumns are ever the same, the intensity of leaf colour will vary from year to year depending on the weather conditions in the previous two seasons. Ideal conditions are a mild spring with no late frosts, followed by a cool moist summer ending with a warm sunny September. The Full-moon Maple acts like a barometer, if the colours are bright, then a vintage autumn is sure to follow. The range of colours on this one tree is quite phenomenal, every shade of burgundy, red, orange, apricot and gold, will appear at some stage of the process, with some green thrown in for good measure!

The trigger for autumn to begin is a combination of reducing daylight hours and cold night-time temperatures. The former is constant, the latter erratic. In recent years, mild weather experienced in September and October has pushed the displays of colour back to late October and early November.

Close on the heels of the Full-moon Maple are the Spindle trees, *Euonymus spp.* There are many species which colour well in autumn, but *Euonymus alatus*, the Winged Spindle and *Euonymus hamiltonianus* are two of the very best. There are specimens of both planted throughout Westonbirt, but Morley Ride in the Old Arboretum and Broad Drive in Silk Wood have the finest displays. They produce superb rich crimson-coloured leaves, which are enhanced by delightful parasol-shaped pink seed capsules hanging from every bough.

When warm October sunshine gradually disperses early morning mists, revealing a

Opposite: Acer Glade

Acer Glade

National Maple Collection in Silk Wood

kaleidoscope of leaf colour still moist with dew, there is nowhere better than Westonbirt. On days like this, American visitors have been heard to say "why go to New England when you have all these wonderful fall colours in old England?" Well, it may not be Vermont, but the Westonbirt Acer Glades certainly take some beating. The original Acer Glade which runs parallel with Specimen Avenue, was planted by Robert and George Holford in the 1870's and still produces magnificent colour today. When the Forestry Commission took over the management of the Arboretum in 1956, one of the first jobs they completed was the creation of a new Acer Glade alongside. Known as Leyshon Avenue, after Ted Leyshon the first Forestry Commission Forester to manage Westonbirt, it is the honey pot for autumn visitors. The glade stretches more than 200 metres, and is surrounded by trees which have been propagated from the original Acer Glade. Most of these are Japanese maples, *Acer palmatum*, and although less than 50 years old, the diversity and vibrancy of colours is outstanding. Clever plantings of larch and pine provide not only an excellent backdrop for the colours, but also the growing conditions required for the maples to perform at their best. As with any plant, maples like to be grown in a way which emulates the natural conditions surrounding the tree in the wild. In Japan, maples thrive on the edge of woodland with taller trees around them providing dappled shade and shelter. This is exactly the environment of the Acer Glades.

Since the creation of Leyshon Avenue, two further collections of Japanese maples have been planted, both in Silk Wood. The first is in The Link, a winding grass path beneath mighty oaks that links Palmer Ride with Broad Drive. Along its length and off into the glades on either side, you will find a fantastic array of autumn colouring maples.

Norway maple on The Downs

Larch in Acer Glade

Acer Glade

Lime Avenue

Although still quite young (planting started in the late 1970's), these maples already rival Acer Glade and Leyshon Avenue for the most spectacular displays at Westonbirt. The overall feel however is very different to that of Acer Glade. The Link, as with most of Silk Wood, is less formal with specimen plantings scattered amongst natural woodland of oak and hazel. To watch these jewels sparkle in autumn sunshine filtering through a latticework of branches overhead, is one of the greatest joys of a Westonbirt autumn.

To the west of The Link, on the far side of Broad Drive, is the official National Collection of Japanese maple cultivars. Started in 1982, the collection now contains over 180 different cultivars, and more are being added all the time. Already the earliest plantings, now above head height, produce a delightful mixture of oranges, reds and golds. Here is it not only leaf colour, but also leaf shape which takes centre stage. From the almost fern-like appearance of the Cut-leaved Japanese maple, *Acer palmatum* 'Dissectum' to the deeply veined *Acer japonicum* 'Aconitifolium' there are dozens of different shapes to admire. At the height of the season, when it seems there are admiring visitors beneath every tree in the Old Arboretum, both The Link and the National Maple Collection are relatively quiet. This is one the delights of Silk Wood. Just a few minutes walk across the valley from the car park, and one can be completely immersed in the peace and tranquillity found beneath its ancient bowers.

One tree which really comes into its own in autumn is the Katsura tree, *Cercidiphyllum japonicum* which originates from China and Japan. This graceful tree produces delightful heart-shaped leaves which turn the clearest butter-yellow colour imaginable. If you are lucky enough to see them against an azure sky, the sight is unforgettable, but its delights do not stop there, for in autumn the leaves emit a mouth-watering sweet fragrance which can only be likened to toffee apples or candyfloss. The scent from this 'arboreal sweetshop' wafts away from the tree for some considerable distance, raising the spirits of all those with a sweet tooth and in search of sustenance after a long walk! Katsuras are a Westonbirt speciality, and there are many planted throughout the grounds. One of the finest groups is in an area called The Colour Circle, just off Pool Avenue.

The Colour Circle is a circular glade planted with more than forty different trees and shrubs deliberately chosen by the Holfords for their attractive autumn leaf colour, including the Persian ironwood, *Parrotia persica* and the sweet gum, *Liquidambar styraciflua*. In the middle of the Circle, both Robert and George Holford would set tables laden with food and drink. Invited guests to their 'Colour Circle parties' would then sit and sip champagne whilst admiring one of the most spectacular landscapes of autumn colour in the world.

It is good to know this is no longer the privilege of just a few. Thousands of visitors now have the opportunity to enjoy the delights of The Colour Circle and, indeed, the whole of Westonbirt Arboretum every autumn. Who knows, some of them may even bring their own champagne!

Acer japonicum 'Vitifolium'

Acer japonicum 'Vitifolium'

Acer japonicum 'Aconitifolium'

Persian ironwood *Parrotia persica*

Euonymus hamiltonianus v.yedoenis

Witch hazel *Hamamelis spp.*

Acer palmatum 'Amoenum'

Viburnum opulus Guelder Rose fruit

Acer palmatum 'Dissectum Seiryu'

Winter

On the face of it, the prospect of walking around an arboretum in winter may not immediately sound appealing. For a start, there is nothing to see, no autumn colours, no rhododendrons in full flower, no hydrangea displays. Well, nothing could be further from the truth. Westonbirt in winter is a magical place, particularly when seen on a cold, bright, frosty day when every branch and frond is clothed in a silvery white hoar frost. On such a day, there is a clarity to the air, a sharpness to each vista, not seen at any other time of year.

It is now that Westonbirt's legion of evergreens and conifers come to the fore. From the exquisite golden-berried holly *Ilex aquifolium* 'Bacciflava' on Willesley Drive, to the stunning Golden Scots pine *Pinus sylvestris* 'Aurea' on Holford Ride, there are botanical delights around every corner.

Two of the most striking conifers at this time of year, are the Serbian spruce *Picea omorika* and the Brewers spruce *'Picea breweriana'*. The former originates from the mountainous region of south-western Serbia, the latter from the Siskiyou mountains of North America. Both are areas of high snowfall, and both trees have adapted to this harsh environment by developing a graceful weeping habit to their branches. This weeping habit means that snow cannot lay heavy on the branches and break them, it simply slides off the tree onto the ground. There are good specimens of each to be seen throughout Westonbirt, but probably the best are in Savill Glade in the Old Arboretum, and on Willesley Drive in Silk Wood.

It is evergreens and conifers which provide the backbone to Westonbirt's shelter, helping to protect the less hardy members of the collection. At close on 140 metres (450 ft.) above sea level, Westonbirt is exposed to south-westerly winds which sweep up the Bristol Channel, so there is a need for wind protection and Robert Holford knew it. He planted Evergreen oak, *Quercus ilex*, English yew *Taxus baccata* and Portuguese laurel *Prunus lusitanica* around the south-west perimeter of the Old Arboretum. Many of these trees are still in existence today, and nowhere is this more evident than along Circular Drive. On the Downs, the wind can be blowing a gale, but step inside the Arboretum and the wind is reduced to a murmuring breeze as it filters through layers of dense foliage.

A winter walk along Circular Drive will awaken all the senses, and no more so than when the air is suddenly filled with a glorious sweet fragrance. For a moment or two it can be difficult to work out just where it is coming from, there are no bright showy

Opposite: Acer Glade

Dogwood *Cornus spp.* at Scots Corner Holford Ride

Weeping Birch in the Enchanted Wood

Illuminated Savill Glade

Norway spruce 'Christmas Tree'

flowers to be seen. Closer inspection, however, will reveal groups, or clumps, of small evergreen shrubs with leathery dark green leaves similar to privet. These are, *Sarcococca humilis* and *ruscifolia*, the black and red-berried Christmas box. Alongside each leaf is a small white flower, insignificant to look at, but a real show stopper when it comes to fragrance.

There are numerous winter flowering plants at Westonbirt, probably one of the best known is Witch hazel, *Hamamelis spp*. There are many species and cultivars to be enjoyed, including the most handsome of all the Chinese witch hazel, *Hamamelis mollis* and its cultivar 'Pallida'. It carries fragrant, frost resistant sulphur-yellow flowers from December right through to March and is sure to lift the spirits of any visitor on a dull mid-winter day. Some of the best specimens are in Savill Glade and on Main Drive in the Old Arboretum, and along Willesley and Waste Drives in Silk Wood. In contrast to the yellow flowers of Witch hazel, the Persian ironwood *Parrotia persica* produces bright ruby-red flowers. These burst forth from chocolate brown velvety casings, not dissimilar to moleskin, in late January. The flowers are no bigger than a small fingernail, but carried in such profusion that from a distance the whole tree takes on a reddish hue. Not to be outdone, *Viburnum x bodnantense* 'Dawn', a medium-sized shrub, produces densely packed clusters of sweetly-scented, rose pink flowers. It is an ideal plant for any garden providing colour and interest right through the darkest months of the year.

A winter walk at Westonbirt provides visitors with lots of ideas to take back to their own gardens. For many, the Arboretum is seen as a living text book providing real examples which can be viewed in maturity, thus giving a sense of ultimate height, spread and attractiveness far better than any book can.

Holford Ride

Acer Glade

Witch hazel *Hamamelis spp.*

Paper-bark maple *Acer griseum*

Winter cyclamen

Salix alba 'Britzensis' Scarlet willow

Ivy in the frost

Snake-bark maple *Acer hersii*

Snowdrops

Leaves on a frosty morning

Helleborus x sternii

It is in winter when many of Westonbirt's more subtle delights come to the fore. Eclipsed in other seasons by gregarious displays of flowers and foliage, it is only now that one discovers the real beauty of bark. Without doubt, the finest tree species for attractive bark is the Tibetan cherry *Prunus serrula*. Its rich mahogany-red shiny, smooth trunk, positively gleams in low winter sunshine. One of the best specimens is in Silk Wood on Palmer Ride close to Willesley Drive. Not far away on Broad Drive, is a group of Paper-bark maples *Acer griseum*. In winter, their flaking paper-thin cinnamon coloured bark looks absolutely fantastic, especially when seen against a foil of hoar frost or snow. There are further good specimens on Mitchell Drive, and Morley Ride in the Old Arboretum.

Another maple which comes into its own at this time of year is the Snake-bark maple *Acer hersii* which has marbled green and grey veining down its trunk. In contrast *Acer palmatum* 'Sango Kaku' has brilliant crimson branches which are so bright, they look positively unreal. There are good examples of both in The Link.

It is not just trees that produce attractive bark, Westonbirt's profusion of Dogwoods *Cornus spp*. are one of the highlights of a Westonbirt winter. There are plantings throughout the Old Arboretum and Silk Wood, but probably one of the best groups is on 'Scots Corner' at the junction of Holford Ride and Pool Avenue. Here, great swathes of coral-red stems interspersed with lime green, blur the eye with their intensity. If you are lucky enough to catch them thrusting upwards from a pure white snow clad ground, it is an image that will stay with you forever.

In the run up to Christmas at Westonbirt, a unique and exciting event takes place after dark. It is called the Enchanted Wood, and rightly so, because for thousands of visitors the experience of following a one and a half mile illuminated trail beneath some of the tallest, oldest and indeed rarest trees in Britain, is pure enchantment. More than 1,000 theatre -style spotlights, some coloured, some white, are trained on to special botanical features, such as the bonsai like contorted stems of *Acer palmatum* 'Dissectum' and the 30cms (12 inch) long cones of the Holford pine *Pinus x holforiana*. In this magical lighting, the trees become living sculpture, casting surreal shapes and shadows across the woodland canopy. For many, the star of the show is a giant 150 year-old Cedar of Lebanon *Cedrus libani*. It's great boughs stretching out into the night sky creates an image which takes your breath away.

As the last spotlight fades and the theatre empties, so Westonbirt begins its winter slumber. From now until the delicate white petalled heads of snowdrops appear beneath the ancient oaks of Silk Wood, it is time for rest and indeed reflection. Reflection, not just of the last year, but of a life that has spanned almost 200 years since Robert Holford planted the first tree in a open field. During that time, many generations of visitors have been able to enjoy the fruits of his inspiration. We, as Friends, visitors, or those who work here, will come and will go, but Westonbirt, with its unique spirit, will live on, giving inspiration and enjoyment for generations to come.

WESTONBIRT TODAY

When the Forestry Commission took over management of Westonbirt in 1956, they found a very different landscape to the cherished one we enjoy today. Limited resources and man power during the latter years of private ownership had led to neglect, with many trees and shrubs in danger of being lost forever. In those early days Forestry Commission priorities were very much geared to saving what was already here. Indeed part of their work was to establish what was here! There had been no inventory of the collection since the publication of A.B. Jackson's *'Catalogue of the trees and shrubs at Westonbirt'* in 1927 and even this had not recorded every specimen. The first attempt at an inventory was carried out by Alan Mitchell in 1968, but it wasn't until 1978 that the whole collection was surveyed, catalogued and an atlas produced. In 1981 this information was put onto computer, making Westonbirt one of the first plant collections in Britain to be managed through a computerised system.

Within the grounds, paths were cleared, weeds and competing vegetation removed from specimens and propagation material taken from specimens unlikely to survive. Gradually, acre by acre, the collection was secured.

Other than the creation of Savill Glade in 1961 and Leyshon Avenue, (the new Acer Glade), in 1966, there had been little time for expansion or development. However in 1969 things really began to 'take off' with the creation of Concord Glade, in Silk Wood. It is said the name comes from the fact that Concorde flew low overhead on its inaugural flight from Filton whilst the Glade was being created. Over the next thirteen years many new features were created. In 1974 Palmer Ride was established, connecting Willesley drive with Waste Drive. The Link, one of the loveliest places at Westonbirt for a springtime walk, followed in 1975 and in 1976 the Native Species Collection was begun.

In 1978 the first formal recreational facilities were built at Westonbirt with the creation of the Visitor centre, (now the Country Gift Shop) and the Café Courtyard. In the following year, in Silk Wood, coppicing of the hazel woodland re-commenced for the first time since the outbreak of war in 1939.

During the 1970's much of the English landscape had been decimated by Dutch elm disease. In 1981, at the far western

Trial of elm clones, Silk Wood in Spring

end of Silk Wood, a trial of elm clones was set up, with funding from the European Community, to determine which clones were more resistant to the disease. Dutch elm disease is not just confined to Britain and this same trial was repeated in nine other European countries. The official National Collection of Japanese maple cultivars, situated just beyond Broad Drive in Silk Wood, was begun in 1982 on a site which had been a Consumer Association trial of Japanese Maples since 1979.

After 1979 development and expansion of the collection slowed down and a period of consolidation begun. The only major change to the landscape occurring on the night of 25th January 1990 when wild storms blew down more than 350 mature trees which crushed a similar number of smaller specimens as they fell. Although devastating at the time, with hindsight this natural 'disaster' was actually quite positive. It cleared the Arboretum of many over mature trees, providing opportunities for new generation planting in the open spaces left behind.

Today, Westonbirt is considered to be one of the finest collections of temperate trees and shrubs in the world. It earns this reputation on three counts, the first being the inspirational quality of its design, secondly, the diversity and rarity of the plants within it and thirdly, the high quality of care and maintenance.

With regard to design, there are few, if any, geometrically designed scientific groupings here. Throughout the Arboretum's existence, indeed ever since Robert Holford planted the very first tree in 1829, great emphasis has been placed on the aesthetics of the collection. The positioning of each plant has been carefully considered, taking into account form, colour, flowering, texture, ultimate size and the open space required to allow optimum appreciation. The end result is a glorious arboreal jigsaw where each piece fits perfectly alongside its neighbours.

The diversity and rarity of the tree and shrub collection is truly breathtaking. There are approximately 18,500 catalogued specimens, made up of almost 4,000 different types, (taxa), collected from virtually every country in the temperate world. Within the collection there are 109 taxa which are either rare, endangered or extinct in the wild. When originally collected by the Victorian plant hunters these plants would have been numerous. However, because of the way man has mismanaged many areas of the world over the last 100-150 years, through deforestation, bad agricultural techniques, urban development etc, their very existence is now under threat.

The most regular comment received by staff from visitors to Westonbirt is praise for the high level of care and maintenance given to the collection and grounds. Teams of dedicated foresters and horticulturalists, assisted by craftsmen and Friends of Westonbirt volunteers, manage and maintain the grounds and the collection throughout the year. Every single specimen is regularly inspected and managed as an individual. Each has its own unique remedial programme of maintenance which can range from weeding to tree surgery.

Conservation, Education and Recreation

However it is not just about making the Arboretum look attractive. One of the Forestry Commission's major objectives at Westonbirt is conservation. There are management systems in place to ensure each habitat receives the optimum treatment. For example, the slopes of the open down-land are still grazed by cattle in the way they have been for countless generations. They are never ploughed, fertilised or sprayed, thereby encouraging a wealth of calcareous flora characteristic of Cotswold downland. In Silk Wood, the grass sward is managed very differently to that of the Old Arboretum. There are few close mown areas, the feel is more natural, grasses and wild flowers are allowed to mature and set seed before being cut. This not only increases the diversity of flora but insect and bird life too.

With such an important collection of trees and shrubs, it is imperative that Westonbirt is managed in a way that will ensure its existence for generations to come. Every year close on 400 new trees and shrubs are planted. Some of these will be replacements for over mature specimens, some will be new taxa to the collection. Many will have been grown within Westonbirt's own propagation unit, quite often from seed collected in the wild. Priority for propagation is given to those plants which are known to be rare, endangered or extinct in the wild. Very often these species will originate from countries thousands of miles from Westonbirt, such as the rare Japanese mountain birch, *Betula chichibuensis*. Sometimes however, they may be UK endangered species such as *Sorbus arranensis*, a whitebeam, which only exists in two glens on the Isle of Arran. The aim is to build up their genetic stock so that progeny can be planted at Westonbirt, sent to other botanical institutions around the globe and hopefully eventually re-introduced into the wild.

Westonbirt does not work in isolation. It has links with many botanic gardens, both in the UK and around the world. By working together, institutions such as Kew Gardens, the Arnold Arboretum in USA and Westonbirt can learn from each other and pool their resources, thus ensuring much greater effectiveness in the conservation of rare and endangered species. In recent years, helping to strengthen these links, the Friends of Westonbirt Arboretum have funded overseas expeditions for staff to China, USA and several countries on mainland Europe.

Another example of this co-operation came after the 'Great Storm' which hit south-east England in 1987. Propagation material collected from scientifically and historically important trees blown down in parks, gardens and arboreta belonging to the National Trust and others, was rushed to Westonbirt. Over the course of the next four years more than 70% of all species were successfully propagated and sapling progeny returned to each property.

Collections such as Westonbirt also provide opportunities for plants to be studied. Research programmes may help to identify cures not only for tree diseases such as Dutch elm disease but also identify medicinal properties beneficial to humans such as Taxol, the anti-cancer agent found in yew trees.

One of the Forestry Commission's main objectives is to ensure that as many people as possible have an understanding of the important environmental work which is carried out at Westonbirt. 'Trees are essential to all life' has been Westonbirt's motto for several years and the aim is that everyone who visits Westonbirt leaves with a greater appreciation of trees.

Each year more than 12,000 schoolchildren visit the Westonbirt Education Centre. Here, they take part in a variety of activities designed to help increase their understanding of the importance of trees and woodlands to the environment. Some of these children may have never entered woodland before. Blindfold trails help them to use senses such as touch, smell and sound when exploring the environment around them and mini-beast hunts help them gain an understanding of the wealth of animals, insects and birds that depend on trees and woodlands. Westonbirt employs a full-time Education Officer who is supported by up to five assistants, all who have formal teaching experience. Most of the activities they undertake with the children are geared to the National Curriculum, helping to support the work teachers and pupils are carrying out in school.

Education is of course not just for children. We all continue to learn throughout our lives. Every visitor to Westonbirt is encouraged to learn more about trees through trail leaflets, interpretative panels, guided walks, talks and workshops.

Schoolchildren in Acer Glade

Much of this work is funded by the Friends of Westonbirt Arboretum who also helped fund the bird observation hide which is situated alongside the Education Centre.

Each year more than 300,000 visitors enjoy the delights of Westonbirt. It has become the most visited attraction in the region, drawing visitors from all around the UK as well as many from overseas. The aim of both staff and Friends is to ensure everyone has a wonderful day out and as a result wish to return time and time again. In addition to the spectacular seasonal highlights provided by the trees, shrubs and wild flowers, there is an exciting programme of events and activities which take place throughout the year. Firm favourites include springtime dawn chorus walks with an expert ornithologist, Shakespearean plays in leafy glades, fungi forays and Father Christmas in his woodland grotto. A leaflet giving full information on all these and many more Westonbirt events is available from the Great Oak Hall and the Country Gift Shop.

It is only natural that a walk around Westonbirt will inspire thoughts on visitors own gardens. The Westonbirt Plant Centre sells an excellent range of trees, shrubs and other plants, as well as the normal ancillaries. Expert horticultural staff are on hand to provide help and advice right the way through the year. The County Gift Shop and our new restaurant are just two of the other recreational features helping to make any visit to Westonbirt a memorable one.

FRIENDS OF WESTONBIRT ARBORETUM

The excellent work of the Forestry Commission is supported in so many ways by the Friends of Westonbirt Arboretum, a registered charity, number 293190. Funds raised by the charity are used to provide facilities for visitors, workshops and materials for school children and invaluable assistance towards the maintenance of the collection.

On your visit you may have been given a map, visited the Great Oak Hall, seen the information signs, been taken on a conducted tour in the Arboretum or perhaps ridden on a wheelchair. These are just a few of the benefits provided by the Friends.

The Charity was set up in 1985 by a small group of enthusiasts. Their aim was to help the Forestry Commission at Westonbirt develop the collection and broaden visitors enjoyment of not only the arboretum, but trees and woodlands in general. Today, the Friends of Westonbirt have more than 13,000 like-minded devotees from both home and abroad.

Subscription income, boosted by the charity gift aid scheme, has enabled the Friends to finance a whole range of projects. These include the publication of maps and seasonal trail guides, which are offered free of charge to every visitor, interpretation and information signs at strategic points throughout the arboretum, and a fleet of electric wheelchairs for the less able, some of which have been donated. Perhaps the most prestigious project of all has been the creation of the Great Oak Hall. This provides a magnificent auditorium for presentations, public exhibitions and includes a permanent information point for visitors. It is also available for public hire. Another major project has been the development of a new toilet building adjacent to the Great Oak Hall.

Some other projects are not so obvious but are none the less vital for the continuing development of this magnificent tree collection. Overseas expeditions, funded by 'the Friends', enable Westonbirt foresters to gather information which helps them nurture and propagate many of the endangered species that exist here. Essential reviews of the collection are regularly funded and over the years many plants have been purchased, planted and maintained. With the next generation in mind, a substantial portion of spending is also directed to improving the educational facilities for schoolchildren.

Westonbirt's 'roots' have not been neglected, some of the material for this guide came from an historical survey of the whole Holford estate commissioned by the Friends, who have also funded ecological surveys.

Much of this work would not be possible without the income generated from membership subscriptions but still more needs to be done. As a registered charity we administer a legacy scheme. Legacies need not be large - after all, it only takes an acorn (and time!) to grow a giant oak. A legacy can be left generally to be spent at the discretion of the charity or specifically to one of the ongoing areas of work - maintaining the Arboretum, education, conservation or environmental research.

In addition to funding projects, Friends help out in a variety of ways, giving freely of their time and expertise. They man the information point in the Great Oak Hall, lead tours for visitors, host and steward major events, help maintain the husbandry by working alongside specialist professionals in such disciplines as planting, pruning, grafting and propagating. There are exciting and rewarding opportunities for everyone, whatever their interests and skills, and of course this offers the chance to meet others of similar interests in the delightful surroundings of the arboretum.

All members receive our quarterly magazine "Holfordiana" which includes a diary of the Arboretum and Friends events and editorial features on many of the diverse issues surrounding Westonbirt. It also includes information on our 'sister' organisation, Bedgebury Pinetum in Kent.

The Friends of Westonbirt treasure our National Arboretum. If you would like to join or find out more, please visit the Great Oak Hall foyer and speak to one of our Volunteers. Alternatively telephone us on 01666 880148 or email: office@fowa.org.uk.

THE GREAT OAK HALL

Opened by H.R.H the Prince of Wales, this magnificent mediaeval-style timber framed cruck building was built by the Friends of Westonbirt Arboretum to provide a meeting place for the Friends, and a hall for exhibitions, lectures, workshops and presentations.

The construction is based on a traditional design using green oak, cedar roof tiles with Cotswold stone flooring, all combining to provide a unique ambience of peace and calm in the heart of the arboretum. The Prince commented that "there is something quintessentially English about the Great Oak Hall".

Modern techniques for heating and lighting blend with the old to ensure comfort. For presentations there is an excellent audio-visual system with a hearing loop.

The hall may be hired for corporate and private use and is ideal for receptions, workshops, and presentations.

It also enshrines the most romantic place for a country wedding, with the arboretum providing a feast of photographic opportunities. Similarly other celebrations for birthdays, anniversaries, and baby naming are popular.

Catering, additional marquee accommodation, flowers and photography can also be arranged. A licence for civil weddings is held.

All delegates and guests to the Great Oak Hall enjoy free access, and parking, to the arboretum grounds, by kind permission of the Forestry Commission management.

For hall hiring information, please contact:
The Great Oak Hall Limited, Westonbirt Arboretum, Tetbury, Glos, GL8 8QS. Telephone 01666 880148, email: office@fowa.org.uk.

Friends of Westonbirt Publication

Compiled and written by
Tony Russell Associates ©
PO Box 32, Tetbury, Gloucestershire, GL8 8BF
Telephone: 01453 836730 Email: mail@tony-russell.com

Acknowledgments and References
Thanks to Barbara Norman for her secretarial skills
Westonbirt School for their co-operation and support for this guide.

A T Lee, *The History of The Town and Parish of Tetbury*, (1857), A B Jackson, *Catalogue of the Trees and Shrubs at Westonbirt*, (1927), M Woodward, *The Trees of Westonbirt*, (1933), S Y Barkley, *Trees of Westonbirt School*, (1952), M Freeman, *Weston Birt a short account of the Manor and the School*, (1977), M Symes, *Westonbirt Gardens*, (1988), D Bown, *Westonbirt, The Forestry Commission's Finest Arboretum* (1990), P Gale, *The Dorchester - A History*, (1990), T Russell, *Westonbirt a Celebration of the Seasons*, (1995), Nicholas Pearson Associates Ltd, *Historic Landscape Survey*, (2001), T Mowl, *Historic Gardens of Gloucestershire*, (2002).

Pictures used in The Friends of Westonbirt section supplied by Friends of Westonbirt
Wedding picture © Sandra Ireland Photography

ISBN 1 899803 18 1

All Westonbirt Arboretum photography is by Derek Harris ©

Pictures used in this publication are available from
The WoodLand and Garden Picture Library
at the address below
Designed and specially published by
The WoodLand and Garden Publishing Company
34 Nene Valley Business Park, Oundle, Peterborough, Cambs, PE8 4HN
Telephone: 01832 270077 Fax: 01832 270088